SEW EASY!
for the young beginner

Other books by Peggy Hoffman

SACRED SONGS FOR JUNIOR CHOIR

SACRED SONGS FOR THREE-PART CHOIRS

·MISS B'S FIRST COOKBOOK

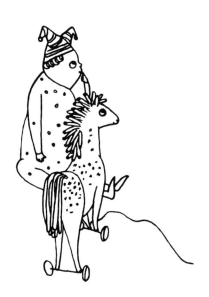

Southwest Photographers Association

Miss B has been stitching around the letters of her name, pencilled on a big scrap of cloth. This helps her to learn to stitch both in a straight line and a curved line. She goes slowly . . . and she watches that her fingers are out of the way.

SEW EASY!

for the young beginner

by Peggy Hoffmann

Illustrated with photographs
by Lloyd E. Jones
Sketches by Susan Perle

E. P. DUTTON & CO., INC.

Tenth Printing, November 1971

Library of Congress Catalog Card Number: 56-5261

SBN 0-525-39185-1 (Trade)

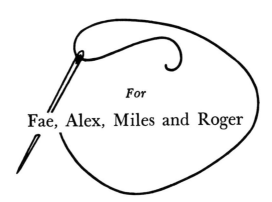

For
Fae, Alex, Miles and Roger

ACKNOWLEDGMENTS

Preparing a book for children takes help from many sources. Among those who have given welcome advice, tried out patterns, run errands and checked the manuscript are Miss Barnett Spratt, Miss Dorothy Dickey, Miss Phyllis Nelson, Mrs. Edward Waugh, Mrs. Robert Overing, Mrs. Clarence Gould, and our families. Dr. Landis Bennett took the photograph on the cover, and Mrs. Robert Barnes cheerfully typed the manuscript. To all of them we say a heartfelt Thank You.

Posing for photographs are Rosemary, Teddy and Bruce Hoffmann, Nancy Nielsen, Alan Parker, Kennye Manuel and Deanie Jones.

Peggy Jones Hoffmann
Lloyd E. Jones

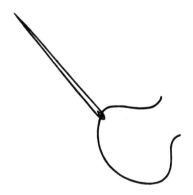

ARTICLES FOR YOU TO MAKE

Apron

Baby's Bib

Beanbag

Change Purse

Doll Clothes

Half-slip

Laundry Bag

Luncheon Set

Man's Scarf

Pajama Pillow

Pillowcases

Ribbon Headband

Sunshine Topper

A MESSAGE TO YOUR MOTHER

Miss B is having such fun learning to sew! We hope that you and your daughter will enjoy adventuring along with us in some of the sewing steps that we have been trying to conquer.

She likes to create something useful and attractive, and if it can also be used as a gift, its pleasure is increased. This is really the basic principle of the whole process of education: fun in doing, fun in the result!

The simple, uncomplicated things come first. She can make a luncheon cloth and napkins with no actual sewing at all, just careful measuring and cutting, then fringing edges. A ribbon headband takes only a few stitches, and she has created something bright and cheerful, and best of all, hand-made. As her sewing skill increases she can make a scarf for her daddy, pillowcases for Grandma, or an apron with huge, glamorous pockets for you! And of course her dolls will be the best-dressed in the neighborhood.

The articles in this book were designed to be made of inexpensive materials, or small amounts. In many cases she uses left-over scraps or feed sacks, so that her experiments in the fine art of sewing will not be costly. Mistakes can be thrown away, if no means of salvaging them can be found, and a new beginning made.

Learning any art requires some outlay for materials, so a few of the designs call for new fabrics. She can do her first sewing of luxury fabrics by making doll clothes from left-over pieces of silk and satin, and at the same time experiment with design.

Because the young seamstress will inevitably want to sew by machine as well as by hand, we have included a section on the basic methods of sewing by machine. Miss B always has help with the sewing machine, to keep the cloth going straight and not too tight, and to remind her not to sew through her own fingers (as her mother once did!). While she is learning, she never uses the machine by herself, but always with supervision.

Let's not forget our boys, who like to learn to do things with their hands just as their sisters do. Sewing is both an art and a craft, as much so as designing and building planes, or constructing log cabins and boats. If they want to sew, let's help them. Every skill that any child acquires gives him more self-assurance and a greater sense of personal security. (Many of the world-famous fashion designers and tailors are men.)

We hope that you will enjoy *Sew Easy!* and that it will open the door to many new and creative experiences.

My brother has taken some pictures to show you things to make and ways of doing it.

Happy Sewing!

SEW EASY!
for the young beginner

Posture

Sit straight on your chair with your feet on the floor.

Have a good light, coming from behind you and shining on your work—not into your eyes.

If possible, put your sewing out on a small table that is the right height for comfortable work. A card table may be just right for you.

If your posture is correct, you won't tire easily!

You may begin your sewing career with nothing more than a needle and thread and a pair of scissors, but soon you will be eager to use all the many trimmings and gadgets that make sewing one of the finest of the Fine Arts. And the most fun!

Always take good care of your tools, and they will work well for you.

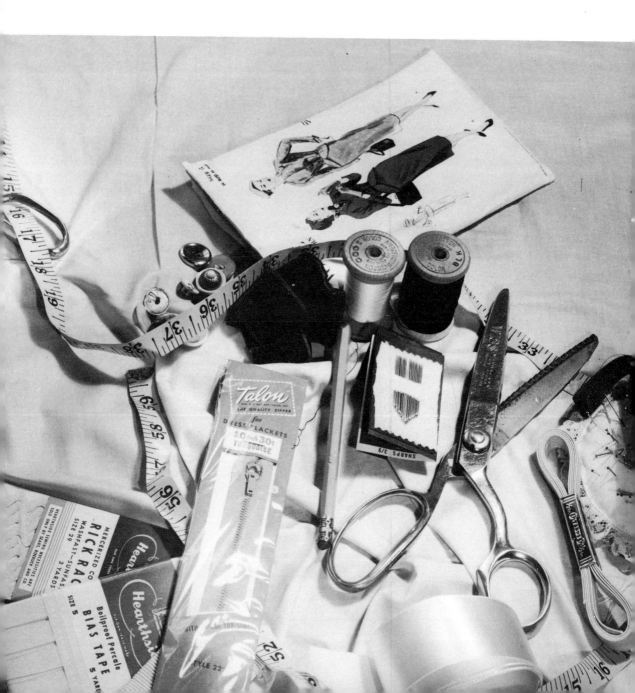

Tools

Any craftsman, cook, carpenter, plumber, gardener or seamstress, can do better work with good tools. Your sewing equipment should be of good quality and in good working order. If needles and pins are rusty and bent, throw them away. New ones are not expensive, and will make your sewing easier.

Needles: Use a medium-length needle that you can hold comfortably in your hand, but that is fine enough to go through the cloth easily. For most sewing, needles in sizes from 5 to 9 are best. For very heavy materials, such as thick wool or felt, sizes 3 to 5 are better.

Thread: No. 50 thread in either cotton or mercerized is the most used weight. You may want to use a finer quality, such as 60 or 70, for very delicate finishes.

Never try to sew with a thread that is too long, or it may tangle. A thread about the same length as your arm is long enough.

Note: Always cut your thread with scissors.
      Never bite it off!

Scissors: Your scissors, or shears, should be sharp and should fit well in your hand. There are many kinds and sizes, some of them designed for special uses, but one sharp pair will serve most of your needs. Pinking shears are especially useful in cutting out the things you will sew because they make an attractive notched edge. These pinked edges are not so apt to ravel and pull out as straight edges.

Thimble: This neat little tool will keep your fingers from getting pricked by the needle.

Pincushion: Keep your pins, and perhaps a few needles, in a pincushion near your work. You might like to fasten a small one to a piece of elastic, and wear it around your left wrist so it is handy.

Tape Measure, Ruler, and Yardstick: These three measuring tools are essential. Always start to measure from the end that says 1 inch!

Chalk: White or colored chalk, or tailor's chalk, has many uses. Mark notches on seams, location of buttons, darts, trimmings. It can be rubbed off after it is used.

Iron: Good pressing is important in your sewing, and often makes the difference between an unsatisfactory piece of work and a satisfactory one. If you are a very young seamstress, you will need some help in handling this tool. Seams should be pressed open as you work, then the whole article given a good pressing when you finish. A steam iron is most useful, but **is not essential**.

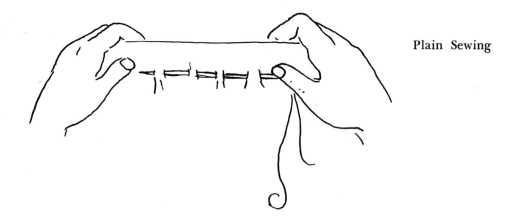

Plain Sewing

To fasten ends:

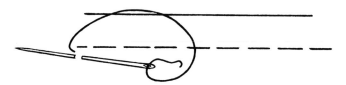

take three small stitches at the
end of your sewing,

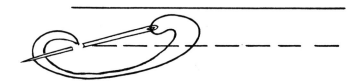

or make a loop knot at the
end of your sewing. Pull up
tight.

Sew around your name with
small stitches.

Sewing by hand

PLAIN SEWING

1. Thread your needle, with a thread no longer than your arm. Tie a knot in one end. It must be large enough to keep the thread from slipping through the cloth. If your first knot is too small, tie another one right over it.

2. Hold your cloth firmly in your left hand (if you are right-handed). Push your needle forward, up and down through the cloth, pulling the thread after it. Try to keep your stitches in a straight line by sewing along a thread in the fabric, or by keeping an even distance from the edge. Pull your stitches up so they lie smooth, but do not make little gathers in the cloth. If you are sewing with your right hand, you will sew toward your left hand. If with your left, sew toward your right.

3. When you are ready to stop, be sure to fasten your thread firmly so it won't pull out. The knot you tied at first will hold that end. You can fasten the final end in either of these ways:
    a) take 3 tiny stitches clear through the cloth, one right on top of the other. Pull tight, then cut with scissors.
    b) *OR*, put your needle through a few threads of the fabric, then put a loop of your sewing thread over the needle. Pull the needle through both the cloth *and* the loop of thread. As you pull the loop tight, you will see that it makes a little knot right in the cloth. Cut the thread with scissors.

4. Your first sewing will be big, uneven stitches, but as you practice you will learn to take smaller ones and to keep them all about the same size.
    Are your stitches in a straight line?
    You might like to practice following curved and straight lines by drawing your name in big letters on a piece of cloth and sewing around the lines.

SEWING WITH A DOUBLE THREAD

You may want to sew with your thread double when you are learning, or later when you need to hold the fabric very securely.

1. Cut your thread longer than for single thread. Your double thread should be not more than twice the length of your arm. If it is too long, it will tangle.

2. Thread your needle, then tie both ends in one knot. Sew just as above. Fasten the end of your sewing the same way too. Using double thread is the quickest and strongest way of sewing on buttons, snaps and other fasteners. (Miss B uses it to sew Merit Badges on her Scout uniform too.)

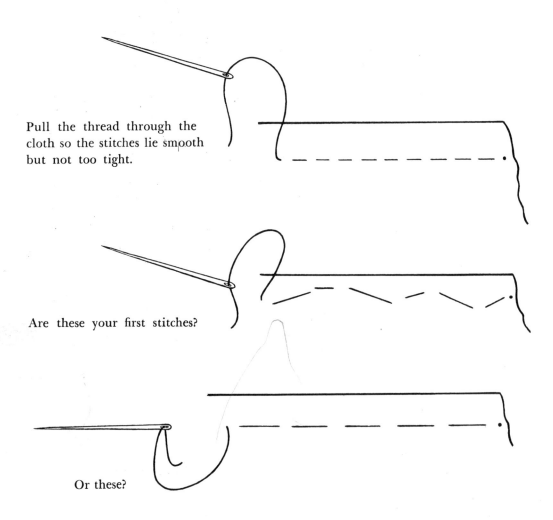

Pull the thread through the cloth so the stitches lie smooth but not too tight.

Are these your first stitches?

Or these?

Here are three pretty things that you can make.

The baby's bib with its handy catch-all pocket can be made from part of a worn bath towel. The luncheon set requires no sewing at all, unless you want to add a monogram or some decoration. The napkins are in a contrasting color. The black and gold apron with its big, big pockets can be made from 1¼ yards of material.

Directions for the bib on page 48, for the luncheon set and napkins on page 22, and for the apron on page 62.

Luncheon set

Let's begin our sewing by making something that doesn't require any actual sewing at all! This lovely luncheon set can be made with careful cutting and fringing. Your cloth and napkins may be all of one color, but contrasting colors are more fun. Make the cloth one color, the napkins another, or one printed and the other plain. Feed sacks make unusual luncheon sets.

YOU WILL NEED

Denim, linen, Indianhead, organdy, or any washable fabric:
in 36-inch material: 1 yard for cloth, 24 inches for 6 napkins.
in 39-inch material: 39 inches for cloth, 26 inches for napkins.
in 42-inch material: 42 inches for cloth, 28 inches for napkins.

WHAT TO DO

1. If the ends of the fabric are not straight, pull a thread to guide you, and cut along it. Cut the selvage thread off very close to the edge.

2. Cut, according to the chart. Napkins and cloth are all square, so they should each be as long as they are wide.

3. Fringe all four sides of each. A sturdy pin will help you pull out the threads. The fringe for the luncheon cloth should be about ¾ to 1 inch wide, and for the napkins about ½ inch wide.

4. The cloth and napkins may be monogrammed or trimmed in some other way, but they are attractive just by themselves. Press carefully.

5. If you can handle the sewing machine, you may stitch along the inside edge of the fringe to hold it. Be sure to sew in a nice straight line. A tightly-woven fabric will not need this sewing.

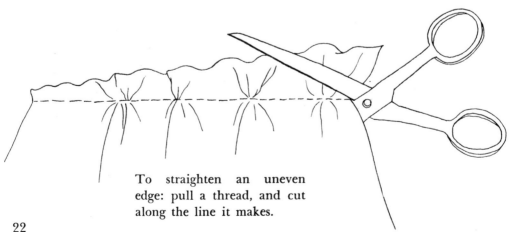

To straighten an uneven edge: pull a thread, and cut along the line it makes.

Luncheon Set

Cloth

Napkins

For measurements, see directions. Each piece is square. Napkins may be made in a contrasting color.

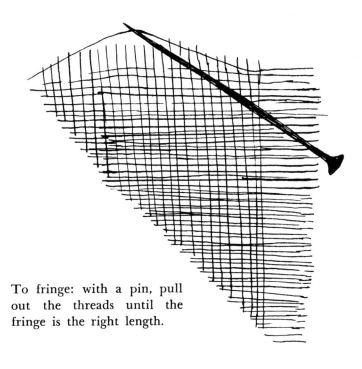

To fringe: with a pin, pull out the threads until the fringe is the right length.

Kinds of hand sewing

BASTING

Basting stitches are used to hold the fabric in place until you can sew it more securely. The stitches do not have to be even in size and can be as long as a half-inch.

Use thread of a color that contrasts with the color of the fabric when you are basting. It will be easy to see when you want to pull it out after you have finished the final sewing. Bastings are always taken out, but of course must be fastened at each end just as in any sewing.

RUNNING SEWING

Neat, small stitches in a straight line. Fasten both ends securely with a good knot in the thread when you begin, and a solid fastening at the end. The stitches should be about ⅛ inch in length, if you can make them that small!

(Or even smaller, like those your great-grandmother made!)

OVERCASTING

This stitch is used to keep a raw edge from raveling, or from looking ragged. Trim the fabric first, to get rid of the loose threads. Sew over and over the edge as in the sketch. The stitches will slant. Try to keep your thread from being too tight.

BLANKET STITCH

Usually done with embroidery thread or wool yarn, blanket stitch makes an attractive edge for many articles. If the fabric is heavy and solid, such as felt, no other hemming or finishing will be needed. The blanket stitch can be put around the edge to hold it and to trim it.

On lighter-weight fabrics, you may hem the edge first, then use the blanket stitch over the hem for a colorful and attractive trimming.

You can make a clever Change Purse out of part of an old felt hat or a heavy piece of cloth, and use the blanket stitch around the edge.

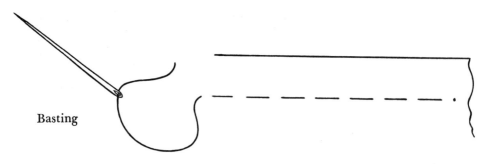

Basting

24

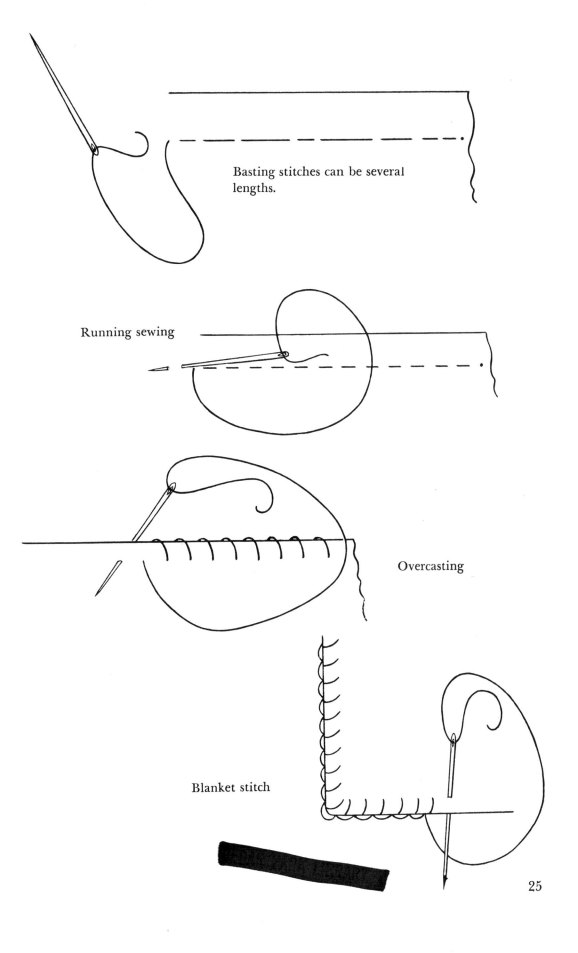

Basting stitches can be several
lengths.

Running sewing

Overcasting

Blanket stitch

25

Change purse

YOU WILL NEED

Felt or heavy wool, about 6 inches by 8 inches.

Snap, or a button, for fastening.

WHAT TO DO

1. This purse can be made from a worn felt hat if you have one. Rip the hat apart. The felt can be made to lie flat by steaming it over a boiling teakettle, then pressing quickly, or by pressing with a steam iron. An experienced adult should help you with this. New felt will not need this treatment. Heavy wool coating can be used also.

2. Cut, according to the chart. If you have pinking shears, use them to give an interesting notched edge.

3. Fold A-B to meet C-D. Sew these two sides together, using the blanket stitch if you like. If you baste them first it will be much easier. Pull the bastings out when you finish.

4. Make another fold at the line C-D, which will turn the top flap down over the opening.

5. Fasten this flap to the purse with a snap, or cut a buttonhole in the flap and sew a button under it, on the purse, to hold it shut. If you want to sew around the buttonhole to make it more secure, see the directions on page 66. If the purse is made of felt, the buttonhole won't need this sewing.

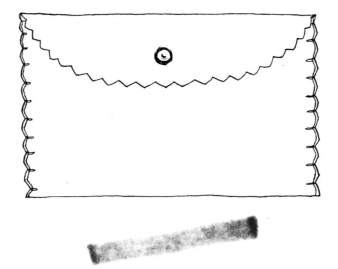

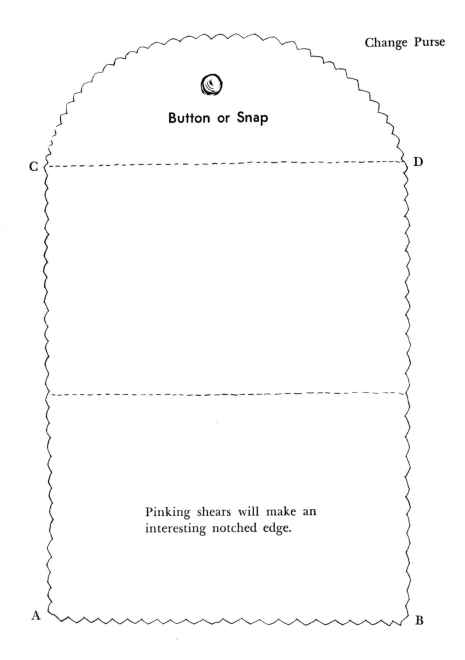

Button or Snap

Pinking shears will make an interesting notched edge.

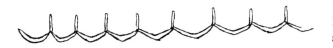

Finish edges with the blanket stitch.

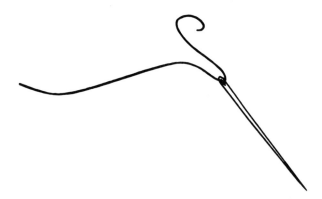

Ribbon headband

YOU WILL NEED

15 inches of ribbon, 1 to 2 inches wide.

5 inches of elastic, ¼ to ½ inches wide.

(If headband is for a grownup, use 17 inches of ribbon.)

WHAT TO DO

1. Using a double thread in your needle, sew one end of the ribbon to one end of the elastic. The ribbon should lap over the elastic by about a half-inch. The ribbon will be wider than the elastic, so make a small pleat in the ribbon to make it fit the width of the elastic.

2. Sew the other end of the ribbon to the other end of the elastic. Be sure that neither is twisted. Try it on for size. If it is too large, fold the ribbon over a little more and sew it down to the elastic. It should fit snugly. The finished length for a child should be about 19 inches, for a grownup about 21 inches.

3. Wear the headband with the ribbon part in front and the elastic out of sight in back, under your hair.

NOTE:

You may make headbands to match your favorite dresses by using a matching strip of cloth about 2 inches wide, instead of ribbon. Hem the edges first, then fasten to the elastic, taking several small pleats in the cloth to make it fit the width.

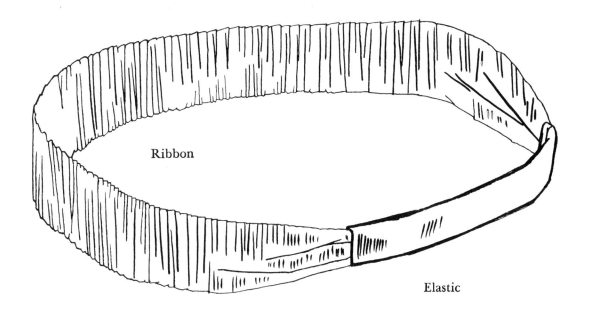

Ribbon

Elastic

Ribbon Headband   any size

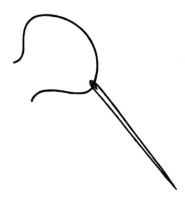

Seams

A seam is the line formed by sewing two pieces of fabric together. The most common forms are the plain seam and the French seam. Learn to sew them straight!

PLAIN SEAM

This basic seam is used to fasten two pieces of cloth together, with their right sides together and the raw edges exposed on the wrong sides. The two edges of the fabric should match. The seam is usually sewed ½ inch to ⅝ inch from the edge. After the seam is sewed, it should be pressed open with an iron so that it lies flat.

FRENCH SEAM

1. This is a double seam which covers up the raw edges. It makes a strong seam for light fabrics that must be washed often.

2. Make a plain seam first, but with the *wrong* sides of the fabric together, sewing on the *right* side.

3. Cut off the raw edges so they are even and about ¼ inch wide.

4. Turn the seam the other side out, creasing it open with your fingers.

5. Fold together again, *right* sides together, and baste the seam ½ inch wide. Sew over the bastings, then pull them out.

6. If a few loose threads show, cut them off. Press with an iron. We will use the French seam to make a pair of pillowcases, for a firm, long-wearing seam.

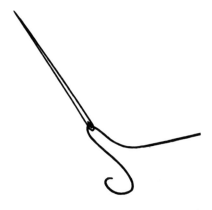

Plain Seam (Pinked edges)

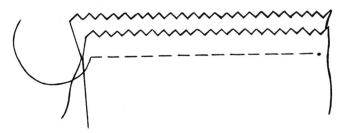

Plain Seam, pressed open
(Overcast edges)

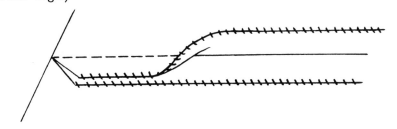

French Seam

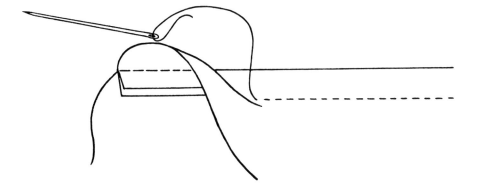

Pillowcases

YOU WILL NEED

1 yard of broadcloth, percale, or pillow tubing, for each pillowcase. 2 yards will make one pair.

Rick-rack, lace, or other trimming.

WHAT TO DO

1. Be sure the cut edges are straight. If they are not, pull a thread and cut along it.

2. If you are using yard goods, instead of the seamless pillow tubing, sew the selvage edges (the sides) together first, using a plain seam, with the right sides together. (Many cotton fabrics do not have a right or wrong side. If you are in doubt about the cloth you are sewing on, ask for help.)

3. Make a French seam at one end. Remember that the first seam in a French seam is made on the *right* side of the cloth, with the *wrong* sides together. Trim the raw edges, turn the seam and crease it open with your fingers. Make the second seam on the *wrong* side of the cloth with the *right* sides together.

4. At the other end, or the open end, make a wide hem, 3 inches wide. To do this, turn the raw edge down ½ inch all around, then fold it under again 3 inches. Measure carefully to be sure it is turned down the same width all around. Also be sure the hem is turned toward the wrong side, or inside, of the pillowcase. Pin. Baste and sew.

5. You may trim the pillowcases in many ways. Miss B (and her brothers!) sewed rick-rack over the hem. You may sew lace on the edge, or embroider a design, or monogram letters from the back of this book.

32

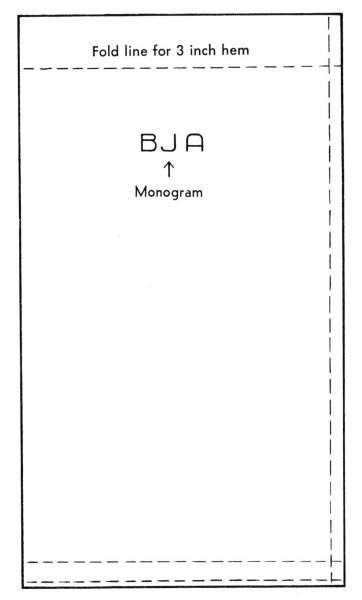

Fold line for 3 inch hem

BJA
↑
Monogram

French Seam

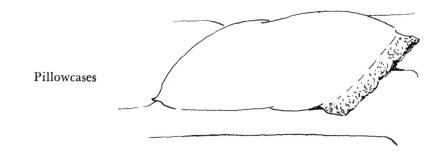

Pillowcases

Beanbag

YOU WILL NEED

> 2 pieces of cloth, about 6 inches in diameter. Flannel, corduroy, denim, gingham, Indianhead, or any sturdy fabric.
> Beans or rice. (Uncooked, of course!)

WHAT TO DO

1. Cut 2 pieces exactly alike, using the pattern or making your own.

2. Put the right sides together and sew, with a ½-inch seam. Be sure to fasten both ends of your sewing securely and to take small stitches. If the seams pull apart you won't have any beanbag! Leave an opening of about an inch, as shown.

3. Turn right side out. Push out the seams with your fingers so they are smooth.

4. Fill with dry beans or rice, but not too full. A little more than half full is enough.

5. Sew up the opening you left, by turning under the edges about a half inch and sewing them together solidly. Fasten your thread securely and cut with scissors.

6. Try several designs for beanbags. If you want to make up your own patterns, watch that there are no little narrow places that will be hard to turn right side out after you have sewed them. Always leave an opening to put the beans through. If you trim your beanbag with embroidery or crayons, do it before you sew the pieces together. To make the designs with crayons, draw them on the cloth you want, quite heavily. Cover the design with clean paper and press over the paper and the design with a hot iron.

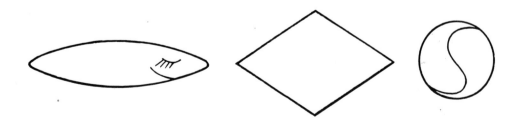

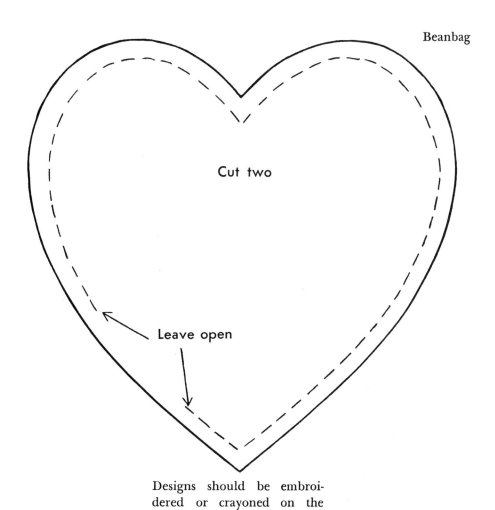

Beanbag

Cut two

Leave open

Designs should be embroidered or crayoned on the beanbag before the two parts are sewed together.

Do you like these shapes?

Use a thin tracing paper to copy the pattern

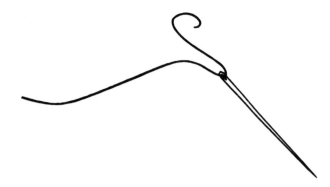

Hems

In making a hem, the fabric is turned under twice and sewed down so that no raw edges show. It may be done by hand or by machine, but most fine hemming is done by hand.

NARROW HEM

1. Fold over the raw edges of the fabric as narrowly as you can. Crease it with your fingers. Be sure it is folded evenly all the way.

2. Fold over a second time. Baste in place. Make sure that the hem is the same width all the way, and keep it as narrow as possible. Use a ruler to help you measure.

3. After it is basted, hem it down as shown and pull out the basting threads. No raw edges should be peeping out! Try a narrow hem on a man's scarf. The apron ties need it too.

WIDE HEM

1. The wide hem is done in the same way as the narrow hem, except that both folds are wider. The first fold should be ½ inch, folded evenly and creased with the fingers.

2. The second fold can be any width from a half-inch to 3 or 4 inches. For a wide hem, it is easier to hold the hem in place at first with pins before you baste. The pins can be moved to adjust the fabric smoothly until the hem is the same width all along. Take out the pins after you have basted. Sew. Take out bastings. The wide hem is used for the pillowcases, laundry bag, apron, half-slip and sunshine topper.

Narrow hem, outside

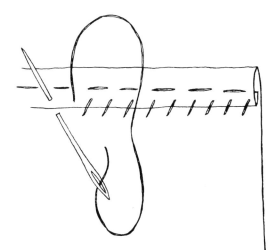

Narrow hem
Baste first

Wide hem
Baste first

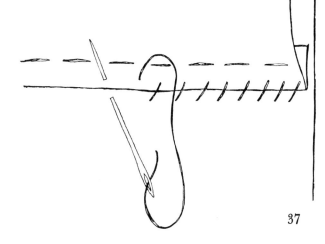

Man's scarf

9 inches (¼ yard) of 54-inch or 60-inch wool: flannel, wool-and-orlon, wool-and-dacron, plaid or plain.

WHAT TO DO

1. Make sure that both of the long edges are straight. If not, pull a thread and cut along it. The short edges, or ends, will be the selvage of the cloth. Cut off this selvage, as close to the edge as possible.

2. Fringe the short ends for about an inch. If you can use the sewing machine, you may sew along the inner edge of the fringe in a straight line, to hold it, but this isn't needed.

3. Hem both of the long sides with a very narrow hem, basting first. Be sure it is even, and that no raw edges show. Make small, neat stitches. Be sure that the bottom cloth is caught in each time.

4. Press carefully, using a damp cloth and a hot iron, or a steam iron. If you are a very young seamstress, you should have some help with the pressing.

5. The scarf may be monogrammed with one, or all three, initials near one end, on the right side. Be sure to keep any trimming simple, as most men don't like frilly things.

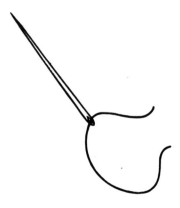

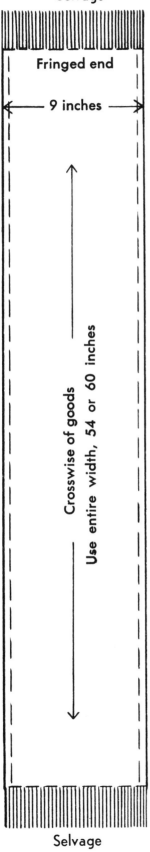

Selvage

Fringed end

← 9 inches →

Crosswise of goods
Use entire width, 54 or 60 inches

Selvage

Man's Scarf

In fringing, be sure the threads at the side are not pulled loose.

Fringe →

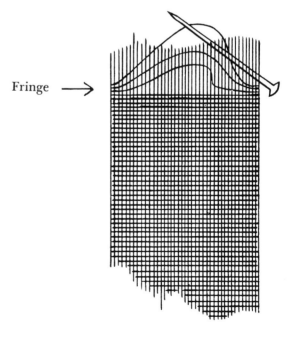

39

What proud father wouldn't like to be wearing a handsome wool-and-orlon scarf that ten young fingers had created just for him?

The narrow hem for the man's scarf is basted down before it is sewed carefully by hand. The ends were fringed first. The directions are on page 38.

The thimble helps to push the needle through the folds of wool-and-orlon.

Sunshine topper

(Halter Top)

SIZE 10

YOU WILL NEED

¼ yard of any washable cotton, or a left-over scrap.
1 yard of ribbon, cotton tape, or cloth to match topper, for ties.
About 1½ yards of ¼-inch elastic.

WHAT TO DO

1. Cut according to chart, making center at least 9 inches. (For a larger size, get ⅓ yard of fabric and make the center measurement 12 inches. The elastic will make it fit.)

2. Sew ends A and B together, with a ½-inch seam, right sides together. This makes the back seam of the topper.

3. Make a 1-inch hem at the top and bottom edges of the topper. The straight edge will be the bottom. Leave an opening of an inch in each hem, to put the elastic through.

4. Take 2 measurements on yourself: one high up under the arms, around the chest, the other at the waistline. Cut 2 pieces of elastic, one for each measurement.

5. Put the piece of elastic the length of your waistline in the hem at the bottom of the topper (the straight edge). Use a small safety pin to pull it through, going in and coming out of the opening you left when you sewed the hem. Put the other piece of elastic through the top hem. Fasten the ends of the elastic together in each hem, crossing them over a half inch. Sew tightly.

6. Fasten the center of the yard of tape or ribbon to the center front, top, and tie the ends around your neck. If you are using narrow cloth strips instead of ribbon or tape, hem them with a narrow hem first.

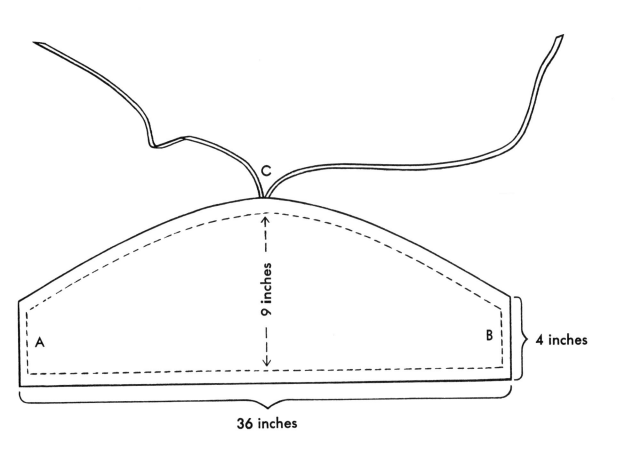

C

9 inches

A

B

4 inches

36 inches

Sunshine Topper (Halter Top)

Bias facing and edgings

Bias Tape, either purchased or homemade, can be used in a number of ways both as a trimming and as covering for raw edges. The special feature of bias edgings is that they will stretch around corners and make a neat finished result.

TO CUT A BIAS EDGING (if you want to make your own).

1. Be sure the edges of the cloth are straight.

2. Fold, as in the sketch, so the end is parallel to the side. The line of this fold is a *true bias.* Cut along the fold.

3. The cut you have just made will be the edge of the bias edging. Measure and mark the width of the strips you want to cut, making the marks parallel to the cut edge.
   Most bias facings are 1 inch to 1½ inches wide.

4. Sew the strips together, right sides together, as in the sketch. Press the seams open.

TO SEW ON A BIAS EDGING

1. If you have made your own bias edging, put the right side of the tape to the right side of the edge to be faced, edges matching. Baste and sew about ¼ inch from the edge.

2. With your scissors, trim the edge evenly. Crease the seam open with your fingers to take out any lumpiness.

3. Make a fold along the bias tape at the width you want it to show. For instance, if your tape is to give a ¼-inch trim, fold it ¼-inch from the seam-line all the way along.

4. Turn under the raw edge of the bias, as for a hem, and baste down to the first seam, just covering the seam, on the wrong side. Sew.

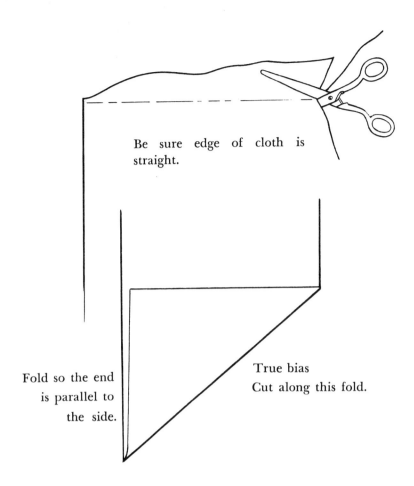

Be sure edge of cloth is straight.

Fold so the end
is parallel to
the side.

True bias
Cut along this fold.

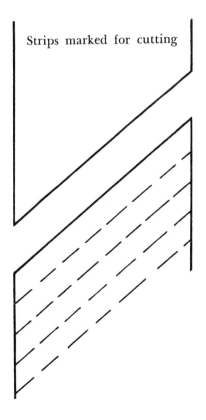

Strips marked for cutting

Sew strips together, right sides together.

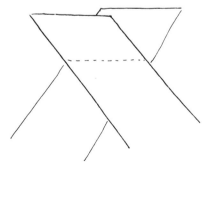

TO SEW ON A BIAS EDGING, READY-MADE

1. If you are using bias tape purchased at the store, fold it in the center. (Some kinds of tape are already folded this way.)

2. To use it as trimming for an apron or a baby bib, slip the raw edge of the cloth into this folded tape. Baste it into place with careful stitches. Be sure that *both* sides of the tape as well as the edge of the article are caught in. Check both sides, and take extra bastings if needed. Sew. Check again before you pull out the bastings.

TO SEW ON A BIAS FACING

1. Bias *facings* are not usually supposed to show, unless they are planned as trimming. For the first step, sew the edge of the facing to the edge of the article to be faced, edges matching, right sides together.

2. Fold the bias over so that the seam just made becomes a *fold*. (This is the difference between the edging and the facing.) The bias will cover the seam and the raw edges.

3. Turn the raw edge of the bias under and hem it down neatly. It will lie more smoothly if you pin, then baste, then sew.

BIAS TRIMMING

Bright-colored bias tapes make gay, easy decorations for aprons, towels, curtains, blouses and dozens of things. If it is used flat, both edges are to be stitched down, after basting in place. It can be combined with rick-rack in many clever ways.

Sewing on Bias Edging or Binding

Edging
Pin close to edges, right sides together. Baste, and sew.

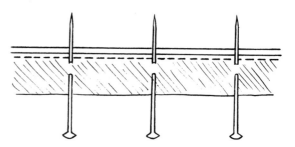

Fold bias over, turn edge under, and sew down, covering first seam.

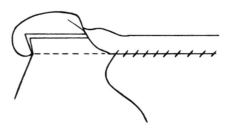

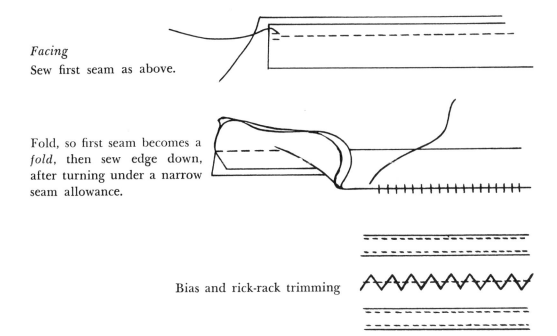

Facing
Sew first seam as above.

Fold, so first seam becomes a *fold*, then sew edge down, after turning under a narrow seam allowance.

Bias and rick-rack trimming

This bias strip will be 1½ inches wide. The first cut was along the fold which made a true bias. Miss B has marked the line of the next cut with a pencil and is following it as she uses the pinking shears. (They are almost too large for her small hands, but she loves to use them anyway.)

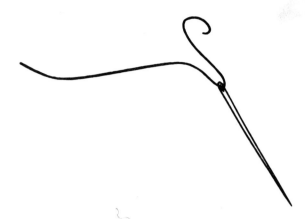

Baby's bib

YOU WILL NEED

Terry cloth, or quilted cotton, 9 inches by 15 inches. (This can be part of a worn bath towel or quilted pad.)

Bias tape in pink, blue, yellow or any cheerful color.

WHAT TO DO

1. Cut according to the chart. It will help if you make a paper pattern first, measuring with a ruler.

2. Starting at A, sew bias binding around the bib, going from A to B to C to D. Be sure that both sides of the tape are caught in, as well as the cloth. Baste, then sew.

   (See directions for Bias Facings and Edgings.)

3. For the tie, use bias tape about 24 inches long. Sew it on the neckline in the same way, going from A across to D. Leave the ends free, and about equal in length.

4. After the tape is sewed to the neckline, sew the tape together to the ends of the ties, turning the ends under to make a neat finish.

5. Fold up 3 inches of the bottom end of the bib to make a little pocket. Sew the ends securely to the sides of the bib.

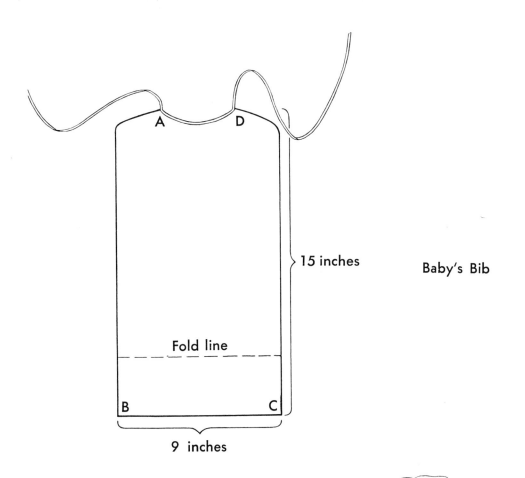

A D

15 inches

Baby's Bib

Fold line

B C

9 inches

Bind with bias tape from A
to B to C to D. Use bias tape
for tie, sewing to bib from
A to D. Fold up on fold line
to make pocket.

Laundry bag

From a feed sack, or a sugar sack

YOU WILL NEED

1 feed sack in bright colors, printed or plain, (or a sugar sack).
2½ yards of cotton twill tape, ½ inch wide.

WHAT TO DO

1. Rip one end of the sack completely open and take out the loose threads. Wash and iron the sack if it is soiled.

2.. If the sack is torn or ragged near the sides and bottom, sew deeper seams there and cut off the ragged edges.

3. Make a 1-inch buttonhole about 4 inches below the open end, as shown. (See Buttonholes.)

4. Make a wide hem, 3 inches wide, at the open end of the bag. The buttonhole should be between the fold and the stitching of the hem so that it makes an *opening into* the hem. This is where the tape is to go.

5. Fasten the cotton tape to a small safety pin and use the pin to pull the tape through the hem, going and coming through the buttonhole.

6. Tie the 2 ends of the tape together, so you can use it to gather up the top of your laundry bag. You may also hang it up by this tape.

7. Trim: You may embroider block letters on a plain piece of cloth in a harmonizing color, then sew this strip near one side of the bag. Or, you can mark these letters on a strip of cloth with heavy crayon. Cover the marks with a clean paper and press the paper and cloth with a hot iron. The letters will stay on the cloth even through the laundry.

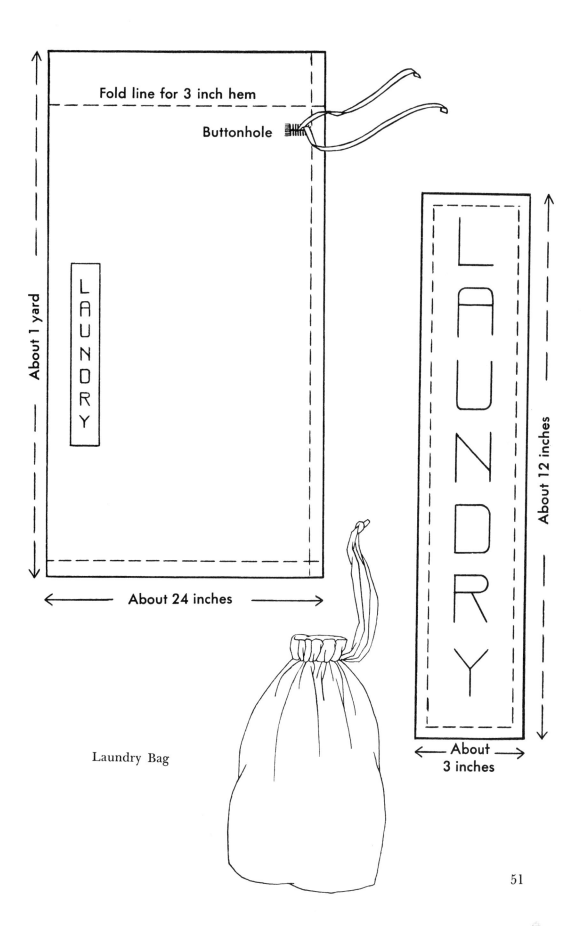

Fold line for 3 inch hem

Buttonhole

LAUNDRY

About 1 yard

About 24 inches

Laundry Bag

LAUNDRY

About 12 inches

About 3 inches

51

Pajama pillow

YOU WILL NEED

2 circles of cloth, 14 inches in diameter. (May be scraps.)
Bias tape, or bias pieces of the same cloth.
Trimming, such as lace, ribbon, eyelet edging.

WHAT TO DO

1. Cut 2 circles as shown in diagram. A large dinner plate will make a good pattern for the circle.

2. Cut from the edge to the center of one circle, as shown, along the straight of the goods. This is to be the opening on the under side of the pillow.

3. Bind this opening with bias tape or with bias pieces of the same cloth. Put the right side of the tape to the right side of the opening, edges matching. Sew clear around, allowing some extra fullness at the point of the cut. Turn. Fold the raw edge under, evenly, and hem down to the first seam, on the wrong side. (See Bias Facings and Edgings.)

4. Pin and baste, then sew the 2 circles together, right sides together, edges matching. The bias-bound edge should fit into the circle, or you may have to overlap it a little. Remove the bastings. Turn right side out.

5. Push the seams smooth with your fingers, then press with an iron. Put your pajamas inside the pajama pillow, on your bed, in the daytime.

6. Trim: Your pajama pillow can be monogrammed, for yourself or as a gift. Or you may sew rows of lace on it. Or make a small rosette of edging, as Miss B did, gathering one edge and pulling it up tight, then sewing it on the pillow. These should be done *before* the 2 circles are sewed together. You may sew lace around the edge afterward, or trim it with sequins from the dime store.

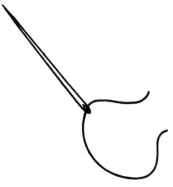

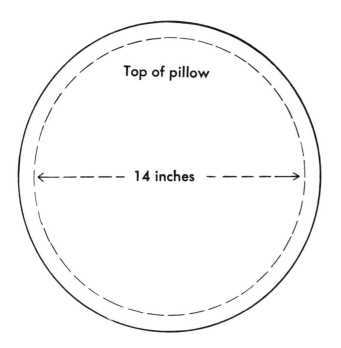

Top of pillow

14 inches

Pajama Pillow

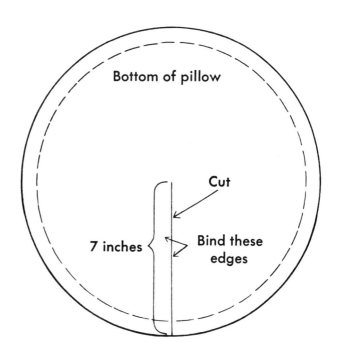

Bottom of pillow

Cut

7 inches

Bind these edges

You can use your pajama pillow to hold your pajamas during the day, and as a decoration on your bed. If you want to trim it with rows of lace or special embroidery, you should do it before the top and bottom are sewed together. Miss B trimmed hers with a yard of narrow eyelet edging, gathered up until it looked like a small rose, then sewed in the center of the pillow.

The pillowcases, which you can also make yourself, are trimmed with rick-rack to match her bedspread.

A half-slip for a fashionable young lady, made from embroidered eyelet. It could be of taffeta or net too. The wide hem may be made into a narrow one as the young lady grows taller. And the elastic at the top will help to keep it fitting her for an extra season too.

Half-slip

SIZE 10

YOU WILL NEED

2 yards of taffeta, net, organdy or eyelet, any width.
Elastic, ¼ or ½ inch wide, ½ inch shorter than waistline.

WHAT TO DO

1. The *length* of the slip will be *crosswise* of the fabric. See chart. To decide the length you want, measure from your waistline to the bottom of your favorite dress, then subtract 1 inch. This is the *finished* length for your half-slip. Now, add 5 inches, to allow for hems. This is the *cutting* length. The chart shows a cutting length of 26 inches, which will make a finished length of 21 inches. A cutting length of 30 inches would make a finished length of 25 inches.

2. With right sides together, baste and sew the two ends, A and B, together, with a ½-inch seam. Press the seam open.

3. Working on the wrong side, make a 1-inch hem at the top. (Turn under the raw edge ½ inch, then another inch.) Baste, and sew in place. Leave one inch of the hem open, not sewed.

4. Measure your waistline, then cut a piece of elastic ½ inch shorter. Fasten the elastic to a small safety pin and use the pin to pull the elastic through the top hem. Sew the 2 ends of elastic together securely, crossing them over ½ inch. Be sure the elastic is not twisted.

5. Make a wide hem, 3 inches wide, in the bottom of the slip. Baste it first, then try it on to see if it is the right length. You can shorten or lengthen it before you do the final sewing.

6. You may sew lace around the bottom. Or you can buy fabrics with one embroidered edge, which need no hem and make lovely slips.

56

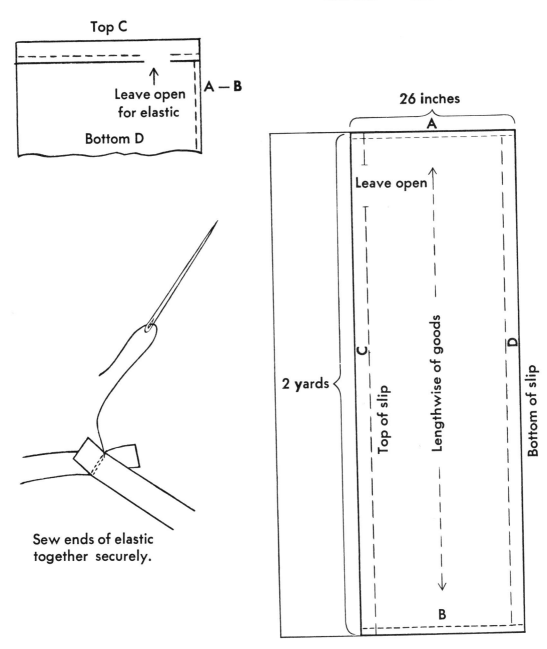

Top C

Leave open
for elastic

A — B

Bottom D

Sew ends of elastic
together securely.

Half-slip   size 10

26 inches

A

Leave open

C

Top of slip

Lengthwise of goods

2 yards

D

Bottom of slip

B

Gathering or ruffling

Gathering means to draw up the sewing thread, making little folds in the fabric. These folds can be pushed along the thread gently, so they are evenly distributed. Ruffles are narrow strips of cloth gathered, and sewed to straight pieces or straight edges of other cloth.

TO GATHER

1. The fabric to be gathered or ruffled should be about 1½ times as long as you want it to be when it is drawn up. It can be as much as twice as long, but no longer or it will be bulky.

2. Tie a good knot in your thread. A double thread is better. Take basting stitches along the edge to be gathered, keeping about ¼ inch from the edge. Leave 2 inches of thread free at the end. Do not knot it.

3. Make another row of stitches ¼ inch farther in from the edge, and a third row if you like. Leave 2 inches of thread free without knotting it when you finish.

4. Grasp all the loose ends in one hand and pull gently. Ease the folds of cloth along with your other hand. A strong pin will help. Don't hurry! If you break a gathering thread, pull it out and put in another one.

5. When the fabric is pulled up to the length you want it, tie the loose ends together, so the gathering does not pull out.

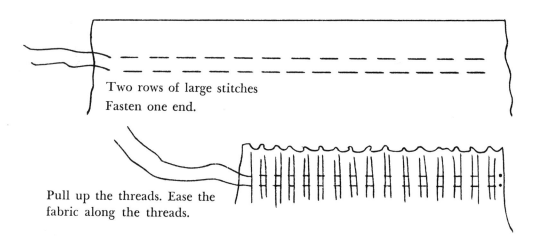

Two rows of large stitches
Fasten one end.

Pull up the threads. Ease the fabric along the threads.

The gathered or ruffled edge is basted to the straight edge before it is stitched. Basting threads are of a contrasting color, so they will be easy to see when you are ready to pull them out.

Work on a table with a good light, and sit up straight!

TO SEW A GATHERED EDGE TO A STRAIGHT EDGE

If the gathered or ruffled edge is to be sewed to a straight edge as in the apron in this book, here is an easy way.

1. *Before* you pull up the gathers, pin the outside ends of the gathered piece to the outside ends of the straight piece.
   (The apron pattern asks you to leave ½ inch at each end of the straight piece for a seam allowance, since it is the belt.)

2. Find the middle of the space between these two pins, on both pieces. Pin the 2 pieces together at that spot.

3. Find the middle of the spaces between this center pin and the end pins and pin *these* middles together. Keep repeating until there are pins every 2 or 3 inches. When the 2 pieces of fabric are pinned this way, the fullness is already fairly well distributed.

4. Begin pulling up the gathering threads and easing the gathers into place. Baste. Take out the pins. Sew!

NOTE:

Always work with the gathers or ruffles toward you so you can keep the edges from getting folded under and caught in the seam. Don't take out the bastings until you are sure the final sewing is correct, then pull out the gathering threads too. It will be easier if you have used thread of a contrasting color for both.

TO TOP-STITCH A STRAIGHT EDGE TO A GATHERED EDGE

Sew the gathers to the straight edge as shown above. Turn to the right side. Press with an iron so that the gathers and the raw edges are both under the *straight* edge. Top-stitch, or sew very neatly by hand, close to the edge.

Pin gathered edge to the straight edge. Baste, then sew. Pin ends together first, then middle.

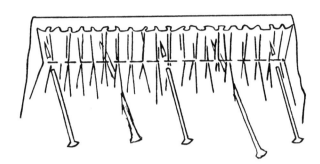

Straight edge top-stitched to a gathered edge

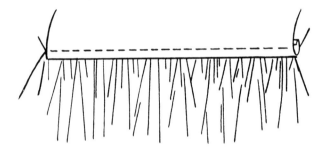

Top-stitching a straight edge with a decorative zig-zag stitch

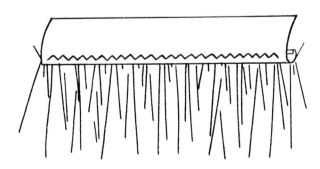

Apron

1¼ yards of gay printed cotton, any width.

WHAT TO DO

1. Cut according to the chart, on the solid lines.

2. You won't need to hem the sides of the apron, unless the selvage is unattractive. Put a 2-inch hem in the bottom of the largest piece. (See directions for Hems.)

3. Make a 2-inch hem in the top of each pocket. Turn under the raw edges of the pocket ½ inch. Pin the pockets in place according to the dotted lines. (About 3 inches from the top and 2 inches from the sides.) Baste. Sew into place, leaving the top hemmed edge free.

4. Gather the top edge of the apron. Pin and baste this gathered edge to the long edge of the waistband, right sides together. Have ½ inch of the waistband extending at each end. Adjust the gathers evenly. (See directions under Gathering and Ruffling.) Sew. Take out the pins and bastings.

5. Fold the waistband in half, lengthwise, right sides together. Sew the 2 ends with a ½-inch seam. Turn right side out and press. One long side of the waistband will still be open. This is to be turned under ½ inch, then sewed down to the wrong side of the apron, along the line of the *first* seam.

6. Ties: Make a narrow hem on the long sides of the ties. The selvage will be one end and doesn't need hemming. Fasten one tie to each side of the waistband, taking a little pleat in each tie to make it fit. The raw edges of the tie should be under the waistband.

7. Trimming can be bias tape, or embroidering, if you like. Your apron may not need any other trimming if it is colorful.

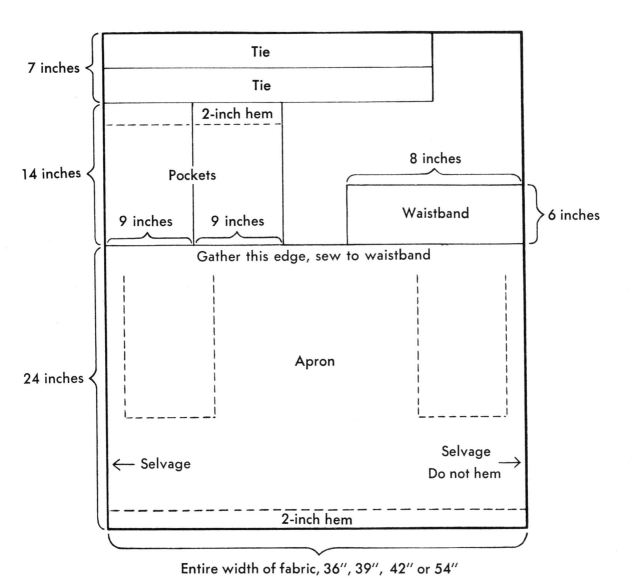

7 inches

Tie

Tie

14 inches

2-inch hem

Pockets

9 inches | 9 inches

8 inches

Waistband

6 inches

Gather this edge, sew to waistband

24 inches

Apron

← Selvage

Selvage
Do not hem →

2-inch hem

Entire width of fabric, 36″, 39″, 42″ or 54″

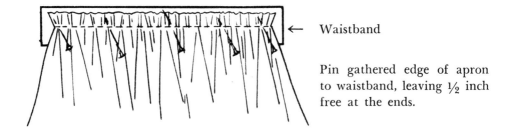

← Waistband

Pin gathered edge of apron to waistband, leaving ½ inch free at the ends.

Sewing on buttons and other fasteners

SEWING ON A BUTTON

a) *Sew-through type.*

1. Mark the exact spot for the button with pencil, chalk or pin.

2. Use double thread, with a good knot in the end. Starting from the wrong side of the fabric, bring your needle and thread up through the fabric and the hole in the button. Pull the thread tight. Make sure there are no extra loops of thread underneath.

3. Push your needle and thread back down through a different hole in the button, or in the opposite one if there are only two. Repeat several times until the button is fastened securely. Fasten your thread on the wrong side and cut with scissors. If the button has more than two holes you might like to try sewing it with little designs as shown.

b) *Shank type.*

1. Your needle and thread will go through both the fabric and the button, as in the sew-through type. However, the hole in this kind of button is in a small shank *under* the button. Your thread will not show on top.

2. Mark and sew in the same way.

NOTE:

If you are going to sew on a row of buttons, make the marks for all of them before you begin, so they will be evenly spaced. Use a small ruler to help you measure.

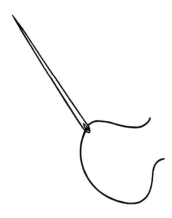

Sewing on Buttons

Sew-through type

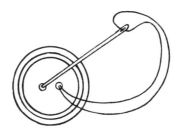

Three ways to make a design
in buttons with four holes

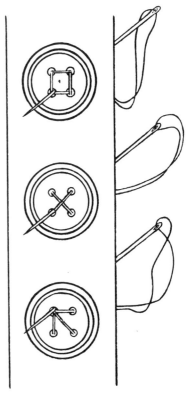

Sewing on a shank type button

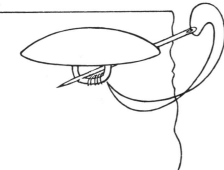

TO MAKE A BUTTONHOLE

1. If there are to be several buttonholes, measure and mark them first so they will be evenly spaced. The buttonhole should be a little larger than the width of the button. Test the size first by cutting one in a scrap of cloth and putting the button through it.

2. Cut the buttonhole. If it includes two or more thicknesses of cloth, baste the cut edges together to hold them in place.

3. Work with needle and thread as shown. (You may want to make your buttonholes with double thread.) The small stitches at the ends are made in the same way as the others, to keep the ends from pulling loose.
Buttonholes aren't easy! You should practice on scraps of cloth first. Make several before you put one in a finished article. (Modern sewing machines have attachments for making buttonholes which are very satisfactory.)

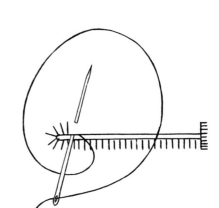

Making a buttonhole

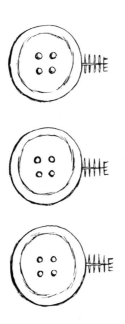

Horizontal buttonhole

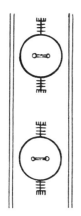

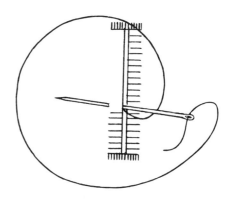

SEWING ON SNAPS

1. Mark the exact spots for both the top and bottom of the snap. Sew through the fabric and the holes in the snap as shown. Use double thread and have a good knot in the end.

2. Be sure to fasten the ends of your thread tightly, on the wrong side. Watch that there are no loose loops of thread.

IMPORTANT:

Be sure that you have the correct sides of the snaps facing each other so they will fasten together. It's easy to get one part wrong side up. If you have sewed on snaps that won't fasten, this may be the reason.

SEWING ON HOOKS AND EYES

1. For a hook and eye, remember always that the *end* of the hook, and not the center, is the part that connects with the eye. Mark the location of the hook first, then mark the spot for the eye where the end of the hook will come.

2. Proceed the same as for snaps. Be sure to fasten both ends of the hook. Pull your thread tightly each time so there are no extra loops.

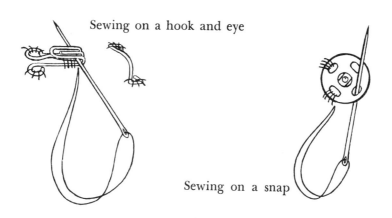

Sewing on a hook and eye

Sewing on a snap

This charming little doll, whose name is Annelore, came to America from Europe and is so pleased with her first American clothes! Nancy is trying on a bright red sash to go with her darker red skirt and sheer white blouse. Directions on page 69.

You can make yourself a headband like Nancy's by hemming a piece of cloth to match your dress and fastening it to a small piece of elastic. Directions on page 28.

Doll clothes

Making clothes for your favorite doll is great fun, because she will be patient while you are fitting her! Your mother will like it too, because doll clothes can usually be made from scraps of cloth. Your doll can be dressed like a queen if you have scraps of satins, laces, embroidered organdies or fine linens. And if you make a mistake, you can throw it away and begin again!

You can use tracing paper to copy these patterns if they are the size you need. If not, you can draw your own patterns from these charts, making them the size you want.

These patterns are for a 7-inch doll. For a 10-inch doll, cut the patterns 1½ times larger. For a 12- to 14-inch doll, cut them twice as large.

The neckline and waistline openings should be cut small until you try the garment on your doll. Usually they will both need a small hem, so don't cut off too much fabric.

Fastenings: The easiest way to fasten a blouse or skirt for a small doll is to sew pieces of ribbon or tape to the two edges to be fastened, then tie them together. Or one length of ribbon can be sewed around a neckline or waistline, leaving the ends free. Snaps, or hooks and eyes can also be used. Buttons and buttonholes do not work very well, since there isn't much space for a buttonhole.

NOTE:
Some very well-dressed dolls have been known to wear their clothes fastened with tiny safety pins that don't show, but we won't mention it here . . . sh-h- . . .

SCARF

Cut a triangle as in the chart. Fringe the straight edges. Hem or overcast the bias edge, (or use pinking shears to finish the edge if you have them). Make the scarf of light-weight wool for her winter clothes, and of organdy or net for more formal wear. She can wear it around either her head or her shoulders. See Man's Scarf or Luncheon Set for fringing directions.

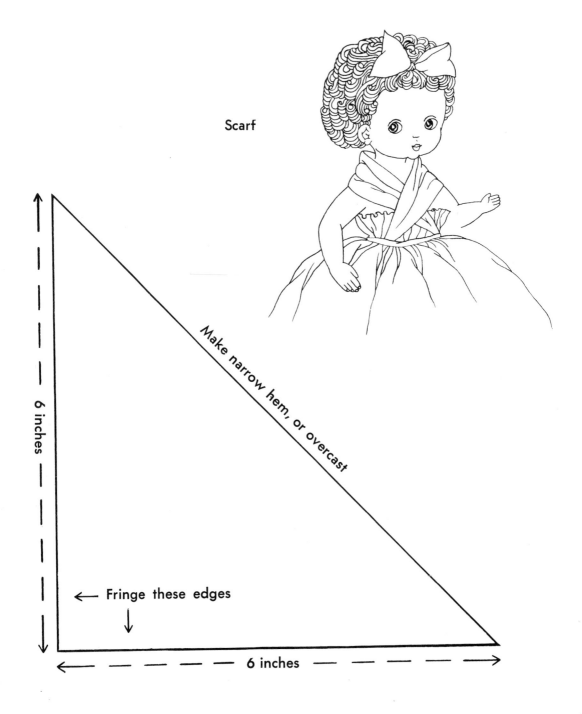

Scarf

Make narrow hem, or overcast

6 inches

← Fringe these edges

← — — — — — — 6 inches — — — — — →

BALLERINA SKIRT

1. Cut out the skirt in a circle. A dinner or salad plate may give you the right size pattern. Cut out the center and try it on your doll.

2. Cut the waistline the right size, not too big. Sew the waistline edge to a narrow ribbon, leaving ends long enough to tie.

3. You can make a crinoline or organdy underskirt just like it, only shorter, by cutting along the dotted lines of the pattern.

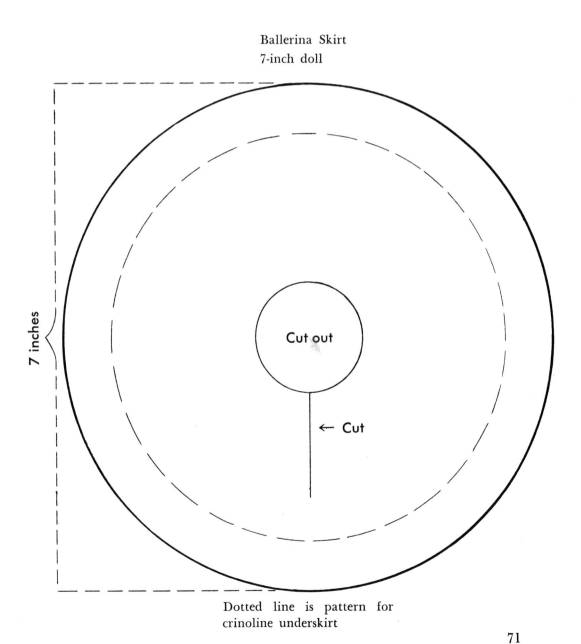

Ballerina Skirt
7-inch doll

7 inches

Cut out

← Cut

Dotted line is pattern for crinoline underskirt

FULL SKIRT

1. Place the pattern on a fold and cut double.

2. Sew up the back seam, leaving the top open, as shown.

3. Put a ½-inch hem in the bottom of the skirt. Hem the top too if the fabric ravels easily.

4. With a double thread in your needle, take basting stitches (or large stitches) ½ inch from the top. Gather it up until the skirt fits your doll's waistline, then tie the ends securely. The opening you have left in the seam will let her take the skirt on and off, and you can pin it shut with a tiny safety pin.

5. If you would like to experiment with *elastic* thread, which you can buy at a sewing shop, notions counter or dime store, find a large needle that the elastic thread will go through. Cut a piece of the thread a little longer than your doll's waistline. Thread it in the needle, tie a good knot. Take big stitches around the top of the waistline and pull it up to fit. Fasten the end tightly. This thread will stretch, so you won't need to leave an opening.

6. Miss B trimmed her doll's skirt with lace. You may like to try many kinds of trimming: braid, sequins, tape, embroidery.

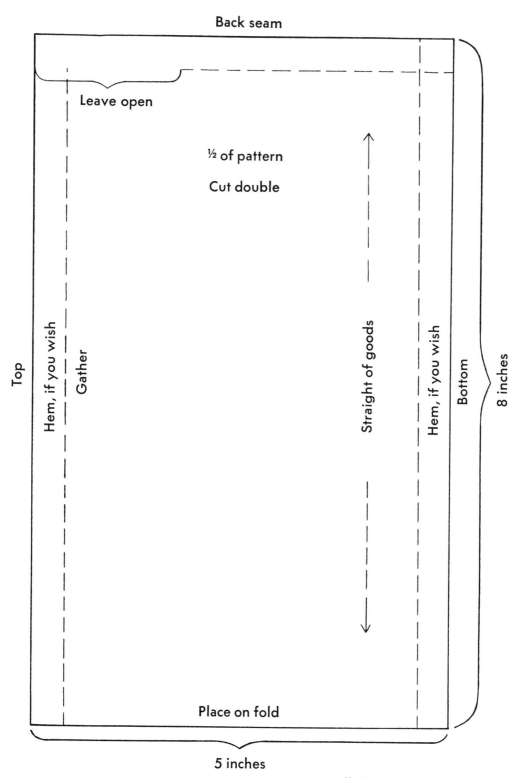

Back seam

Leave open

½ of pattern

Cut double

Top

Hem, if you wish

Gather

Straight of goods

Hem, if you wish

Bottom

8 inches

Place on fold

5 inches

Full Skirt   7-inch doll

BLOUSE

1. Place the pattern on a fold and cut double. Cut it open in the back, as shown in the chart.

2. Sew A-B edge to C-D edge, to make sleeve.

3. Sew a small tuck in the blouse front so it will fit well. Try the blouse on your doll. Cut the neck to fit, but not too large.

4. Hem the neck with a very narrow hem.

5. With a double thread in your needle, make gathers along the cuff of the sleeve. Fasten your thread tightly when you have pulled up the gathers to fit. Be sure that your doll can get her hand through! You can fasten the neck of the blouse with snaps or tiny pins.

6. For dress-up clothes, make a blouse and skirt to match. For evening clothes, make them of luxury fabrics. Tie a ribbon sash at her waist, and pin tiny flowers in her hair.

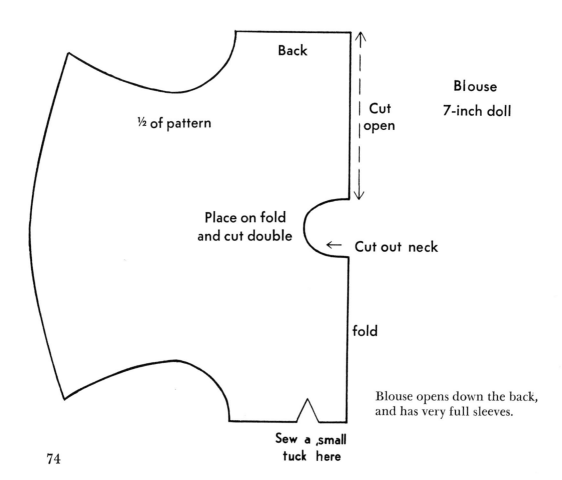

Back

Blouse
7-inch doll

½ of pattern

Cut
open

Place on fold
and cut double

← Cut out neck

fold

Blouse opens down the back,
and has very full sleeves.

Sew a small
tuck here

HAT

1. Cut 2 pieces exactly alike. One is to be the lining, so they may be of 2 different fabrics, but the colors should look well together. The hat might match the fly-away coat.

2. Sew the 2 pieces together, right sides together. Leave the center open.

3. Turn right side out. Press with a warm iron.

4. Sew the center edges together neatly. You may make the opening larger, of course. It should fit your own doll, and not be either too large or too small.

5. Fasten a piece of ribbon at each side of the back and tie the ribbons together under her chin. You will have many ideas for clever trimming on the hat.

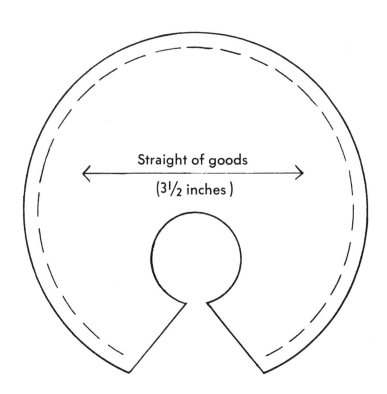

Straight of goods

(3½ inches)

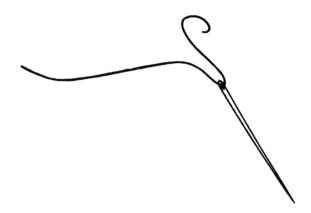

FLY-AWAY COAT

1. Place the pattern on a fold, and cut double, as shown.

2. Cut the front open, as shown. Try the coat on your doll. If the neckline is much too small, cut some of it out.

3. Right sides together, sew A-B to C-D to make a sleeve. Hem the end of the sleeve.

4. Hem the bottom of the coat and put a small hem in the front opening. (If the coat is of felt, it will not need any hems.)

5. Cut 2 pockets and hem the tops. Turn the edges under neatly. Baste and sew the pockets in place, on the dotted lines.

6. The fly-away coat may be worn loose, or you may like a tie-belt for extra glamour. It doesn't need any fastening. It should be left untrimmed so it will look expensive and straight-from-Paris.

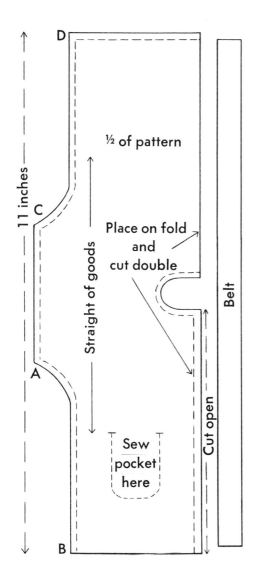

D

↑
11 inches
↓

C

A

B

½ of pattern

Straight of goods

Place on fold
and
cut double

Sew
pocket
here

Cut open

Belt

Fly-away coat
7-inch doll

Pocket

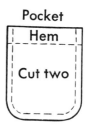

Hem

Cut two

PANTIES

1. Cut according to the pattern, putting the bottom line on a fold of cloth.
2. Sew the sides together, and try it on your doll.
3. Hem the legs and top. Sew lace around them if you like.
4. You may fasten the panties with a small safety pin, or, you can sew elastic thread through the top, using a needle with a large eye, and tying the ends of the elastic thread together when you finish. See directions under Full Skirt.

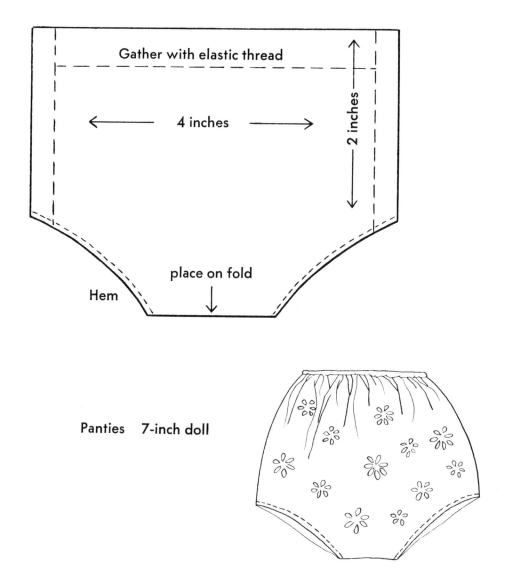

Gather with elastic thread

4 inches

2 inches

place on fold

Hem

Panties 7-inch doll

POCKETBOOK

1. Cut a circle of cloth, using a stiff fabric such as taffeta.

2. If the threads on the edge pull out too easily, you can hem the edges with a neat, narrow hem.

3. Using a needle with a large eye, thread it with bright-colored embroidery thread. Sew around the circle as shown. Take large stitches. Leave several inches of thread loose at each end.

4. Pull up the thread and tie it in a single knot to hold it. Tie the 2 ends of the thread together in a knot. This will make a loop that she can put over her arm so she can carry her purse.

← 3 to 4 inches →

Pocketbook   7-inch doll

Sewing by machine

The sewing machine is one of the most fascinating inventions, and it is constantly being improved. If you enjoy sewing, you will want to learn to sew by machine. Learn to run it properly. Take good care of it and it will serve you faithfully!

Some older, experienced person should help you with the sewing machine until you can handle it safely by yourself. Different models of sewing machines have different methods of threading and of stitching, so our directions will be rather general, but your mother, teacher, Scout or Camp-fire leader, or some good neighbor can show you how to handle the one that you will use.

1. Learn how to thread the machine, top and bottom. Learn how to wind the bobbin and put it in its proper place.

2. Practice putting the presser foot up and down. It must always be *down* when you are stitching, *up* when you are putting cloth in or out. The *needle* must be free of the cloth also.

3. Without any thread in the machine, practice starting and stopping. Learn how to make it go. Can you keep it running slowly without jerking?
   The power that runs the sewing machine is usually in a motor which you will run by a foot pedal or a knee pedal. But the power might be all in your own foot! Some sewing machines do not have motors on them, and their power comes from a foot pedal which you push up and down.
   You will soon learn that you can control the speed of the machine by pressing harder on the foot or knee pedal if you want it to go faster, or not so hard if you want to slow down. Keep your fingers away from the needle!

4. When you have learned to keep the machine going, but *not too* fast, try some real stitching with thread in the top and bottom. Ask the person who is helping you to be sure that the threading is right, so the thread won't snarl.
   Can you stitch in a straight line?

Miss B's mother's hands are guiding hers as she learns to sew by machine. This sewing machine has a zig-zag stitch, and she is using it to stitch over basting threads.

Always keep your fingers away from the needle. Always!

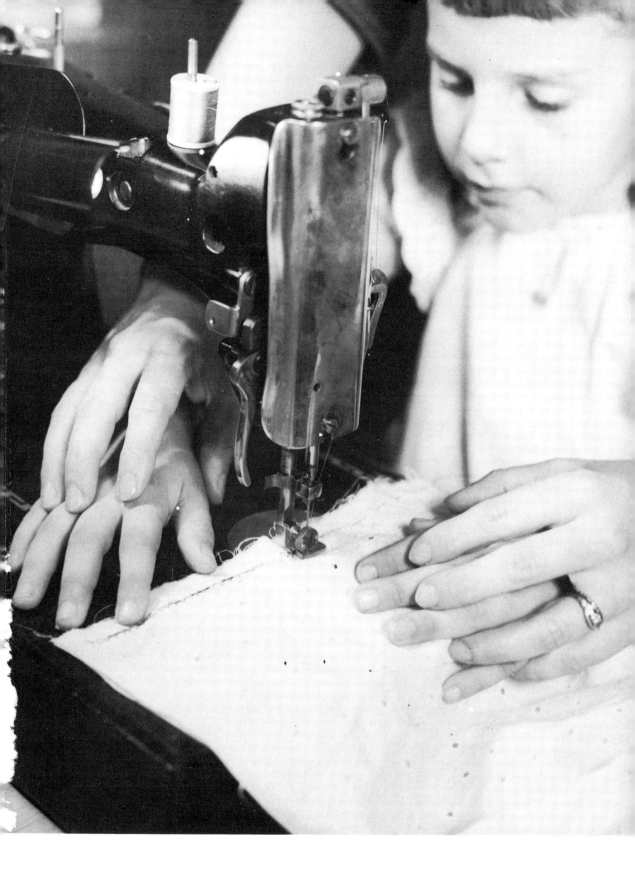

5. You might like to practice stitching on curves and straight lines and even turning corners, on scraps of cloth. Print your name, or some simple pattern, in a large design on a scrap of cloth. Stitch around it. Don't hurry! *To turn a corner*: Stop with the needle *in* the cloth at the place you want to turn. Lift the presser foot, but be sure the needle stays in the cloth. Turn the cloth the way you want to go next. Put the presser foot back down, and begin sewing.

6. If your machine will stitch backward as well as forward, have your teacher or your mother show you how this is done. It will save you much time, especially in tying ends. It can also be used for mending, by sewing back and forth over torn places. (Not many people really like to mend, but when you can do it this easy way, it's almost fun!)

7. If your machine has a book of directions with it, keep it handy. It will tell you where and when to oil the machine. This is important, in order to keep it working well.

IMPORTANT:

Keep your fingers away from the needle! It might stitch *you!* We're going to tell you this over and over . . . we don't want you to get hurt and spoil your fun!

The presser foot must be *down* when you are stitching and *up* when you take the cloth out. Here Miss B is learning to turn a corner by stitching to the corner, stopping with the needle in the cloth, lifting the presser foot, then turning the cloth. When she is ready to go in the new direction, she will put the presser foot back down and begin to stitch again.

Kinds of machine stitching

TO TIE ENDS

Most modern sewing machines stitch backward as well as forward. If yours does, you can fasten the ends of your stitching without any other tying.

At the beginning, stitch forward about a half inch. Stop. Stitch backward over the same stitches. Stop. Stitch forward again and proceed.

At the end, stitch to the end of the seam. Stop. Stitch backward about a half inch. Stop. Stitch forward again to the end of the seam. Cut the ends of the thread with scissors.

If you do not have this type of sewing machine, be sure to leave about 2 inches of thread at both the beginning and the end of stitching. Tie top and bottom threads together by hand. Cut.

TO GATHER OR RUFFLE BY MACHINE

Many machines have a ruffler attachment, with directions for its use in the booklet that came with it. If you do not have or do not want to use this attachment, you can gather or ruffle this way:

1. Turn the stitch adjustment to the longest stitch.

2. Fasten the first end of your stitching either by going back and forth, or by leaving long ends to tie.

3. Stitch with the longest stitch, about ¼ inch from the edge. Leave several inches of thread loose at the end. Add a second and third row of stitching, always leaving a long end loose. Be sure the *first* ends are tied.

4. Hold the cloth in one hand. With the other hand, take the *top* threads in each row and pull tight. Adjust the fullness carefully. Push gently with a pin. Tie the loose ends together.

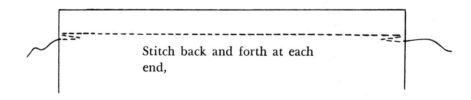

Stitch back and forth at each end,

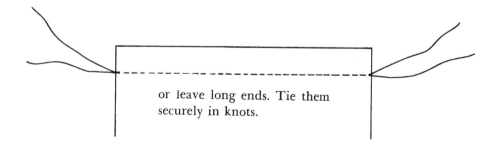

or leave long ends. Tie them
securely in knots.

Gathering or Ruffling by Machine

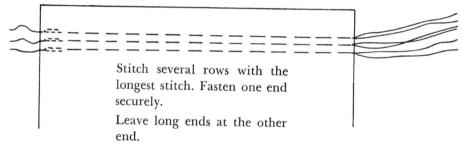

Stitch several rows with the
longest stitch. Fasten one end
securely.

Leave long ends at the other
end.

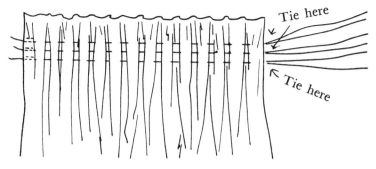

Pull up gathers by holding
loose ends and pushing cloth
along the tightened thread.
Tie ends securely.

TOP-STITCHING

Sometimes called Trim-Stitching, this must be done neatly because it is supposed to show. It is used to sew on pockets, to fasten a straight edge to a ruffled or gathered edge, to sew on rick-rack, braid, tape and other trimmings. The important thing is to keep it straight.

Use the edge of the presser foot to guide your work. Your machine may have an edge-stitcher which can be fastened near the presser foot to help keep the fabric in a straight line. If it does, your book of directions will show you.

Top-Stitching can be made extra attractive by stitching in thread of a contrasting color to the fabric. Try it around the edge of a luncheon set.

THE ZIG-ZAG STITCH

European sewing machines have been built with the zig-zag stitch for a number of years, but American-made machines do not all have it. It has numerous practical uses, and the seamstress who has the use of a zig-zag machine has many sewing adventures ahead of her. It can be used for trimming, making buttonholes, sewing on buttons, applique, monogramming, sewing on lace, hemming, mending, and in many other ways.

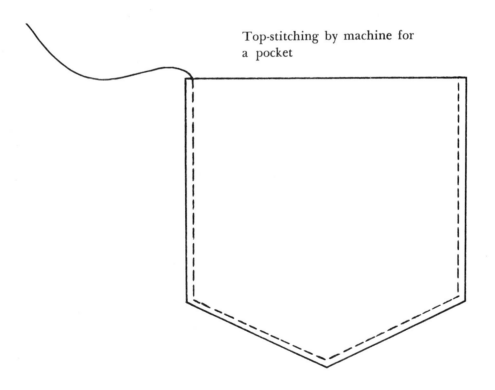

Top-stitching by machine for a pocket

Don't sew if you are tired and things go wrong. Put your sewing away and go out and have fun with your friends! A sunshine topper which you have made for yourself will help you enjoy the sunshine. Miss B made this one in a bright printed cotton.

Which do you like best, these
tall skinny letters or the short
fat ones?

Do your initials make a pretty
design?

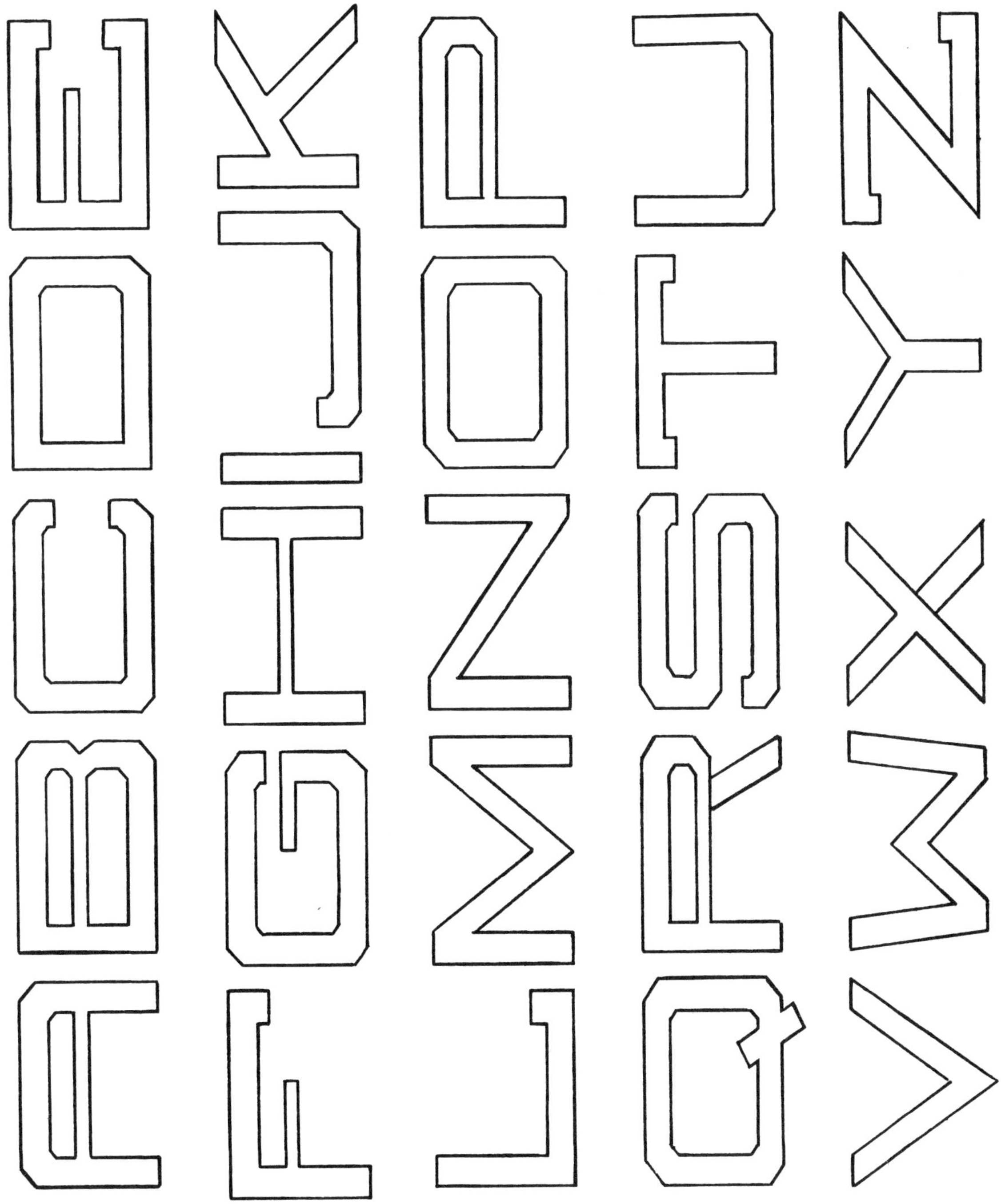

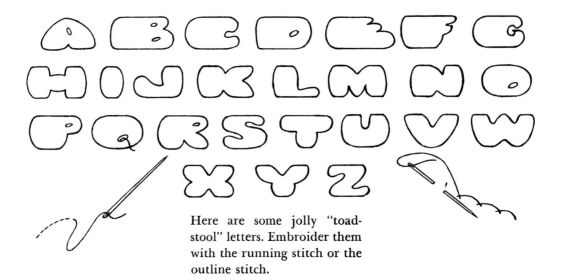

Here are some jolly "toad-stool" letters. Embroider them with the running stitch or the outline stitch.

How did these boys get in here? Maybe they like to sew, too! Can *you* sew on a button so it will stay? Have you tried top-stitching some braid or rick-rack on a special gift for that special grandma?

Let's tiptoe away before these fellows see us and stop working!

INDEX